W9-AJT-566

WHAT'S FOR LUNCH?

WHAT'S FOR LUNCH?

THE EATING HABITS OF SEASHORE CREATURES

BY SAM AND BERYL EPSTEIN
WITH MICHAEL SALMON, Ph.D.

ILLUSTRATED BY WALTER GAFFNEY-KESSEL

Macmillan Publishing Company
New York

*"Does the song of the sea end at the shore
or in the hearts of those who listen?"*
—*Kahlil Gibran*

Lovingly dedicated to Pauline and Bill
W.G.-K.

Macmillan Publishing Company
866 Third Avenue, New York, N.Y. 10022
Collier Macmillan Canada, Inc.

Printed in the United States of America
10 9 8 7 6 5 4 3 2 1

Library of Congress Cataloging in Publication Data
Epstein, Sam, date.
What's for lunch?

Summary: Describes the ways in which
seagulls, crabs, snails, jellyfish, corals, and
other seashore creatures find their food.
1. Seashore biology—Juvenile literature.
2. Animals—Food—Juvenile literature. [1. Sea-
shore biology. 2. Animals—Food habits]
I. Epstein, Beryl Williams, date.
II. Salmon, Michael. III. Gaffney-Kessel,
Walter, ill. IV. Title.
QH95.7.E67   1985   591.92   85-4964
ISBN 0-02-733500-3

· Contents ·

If you go to the beach for a picnic lunch, you probably take along sandwiches and the rest of the food you want to eat. But all the creatures you might see there eat what they find right on the beach or in the water. They have different ways of finding and eating their food. Some might surprise you.

SEAGULLS·

That seagull paddling in the shallow water is searching the bottom for something to eat. If it sees a clam half covered by sand, it ducks underwater to grab it in its beak. But the soft body the seagull wants to eat is inside the clam's shells. Those two shells are very hard and are tightly clamped together.

Do you know how the seagull gets at the clam's soft body? With the clam still in its beak, the bird flies up into the air. There it opens its beak and lets the clam fall to the ground. The seagull flies down after it.

If the clam lands on a rock or some other hard surface, the shells usually break. Then the seagull can eat the meat inside.

But if the clam lands on soft sand or grass, its shells may not even crack. Then the seagull picks it up, flies back into the air with it, and drops it again. The bird may do that three or even four times. But if the clam still has not broken open, the seagull finally gives up and flies off to look for something else to eat.

A seagull seldom has trouble finding a meal, because it eats so many different foods. It eats other birds' eggs and even their babies if it finds them unprotected. It eats worms and grubs from freshly plowed fields near the sea. It eats garbage from a nearby garbage dump. It eats whatever fishermen throw away when they are cleaning fish. And when the tide ebbs, leaving a stretch of damp sand along the water's edge, it gobbles up whatever is lying on that sand—a dead crab, perhaps, or a smelly dead fish.

There are several kinds of seagulls. Some measure no more than fifteen inches from the tip of their beak to the tip of their tail. Others are twice that size. Some are all white. Others are white with black wing tips. Still others are white with dark wings and a dark back. But all of them have big appetites. So can you guess why, in many places, there is a law against harming seagulls? It is because, by eating so many kinds of foods, they help keep beaches and harbors clean.

·OSPREYS

Many birds are a lot fussier about their food than seagulls are. The osprey is one of them. It can eat frogs, snakes, and lizards if fish are scarce, but fresh-caught fish is its favorite food.

The osprey, sometimes called the fish hawk, is a large bird. Its spread wings may measure as much as six feet across. It soars high in the air on those great wings, its sharp eyes searching the water below.

The instant it sights a fish, it flies downward at high speed. Its legs thrust forward just before it reaches the water. Then its powerful talons plunge beneath the surface, reaching for its prey. It makes a successful catch in about half of these dramatic dives.

With a fish in its talons, the osprey flies back up into the air. Then it heads for its nest at the top of a dead tree or telephone pole, or on some other high place. Often it is taking the fish to its young.

When young ospreys are able to fly, they follow their parents to the fish-hunting places. One parent catches a fish and flies into the air with it. Circling around the young birds, it teases them with the fish—and then drops it. The young birds dive downward, trying to catch the fish.

After following a dropped fish into the water several times, a young osprey learns that it can catch its own food. But at first it usually catches a fish only once in every four or five dives.

TERNS

Did you ever hear a lot of loud, high-pitched screaming when you were near the water? If you did, you probably were hearing a flock of the fish-hunting birds called terns.

Terns are small birds, only about twelve inches long from their head to their tail. They fly swiftly on their graceful, pointed wings. They dart back and forth, up and down, and swoop in circles. And they scream almost constantly.

When a tern sights a school of small fish in the water below, it halts its swift flight. For a moment it seems to hang in the air, its wings beating rapidly. Then, like an arrow, it dives headfirst into the water. It may completely disappear under the surface. But in another instant it comes up again, usually holding a fish in its bright red beak.

If the tern doesn't take its catch to its young, it likes to swallow it immediately. But if the tern has caught the fish crosswise in its beak, it cannot. In that case, it drops the fish, dives after it, and snatches it out of the air before the fish reaches the water. This time the tern makes sure to take its catch lengthwise in its beak, so that it can be easily swallowed.

Terns know that schools of small fish often appear in the shallow water covering a sandbar. There the small fish are safe from the larger fish that eat them. But when small fish are chased by big fish in deep water, they try to escape by crowding close to the surface. So terns often hunt over deep water, too, and people fishing for large fish are always happy to see them. A flock of terns diving for small fish in deep water is a signal that there are large fish below.

· P E L I C A N S ·

Pelicans are big birds that nest near warm southern waters. Some measure as much as ten feet between the tips of their widespread wings. Such big birds need a lot of food, and pelicans have to be good fish catchers to get enough. They are.

Pelicans have a remarkable fish-catching beak. Its upper part is long and pointed, like the beaks of many fish-catching birds. But from the lower part of the beak hangs a sort of sack, made of tough skin. This sack is big enough to hold more than two gallons of water.

A pelican looks for a school of fish as it paddles through the water with its webbed feet or flies above it. As soon as it sights one, it plunges straight into the water and opens its beak wide. Fish and water are both scooped into its sack. Then the pelican closes its beak, raises its head above water, and points the beak upward.

Water flows out of the sack through the small opening where the upper and lower parts of the beak join. But fish can't get through that opening. They are trapped in the sack.

The pelican may swallow the fish on the spot. Or it may carry them in the sack to the baby pelicans in its nest. There it opens its beak, and the young birds poke their heads into the sack to get their meal.

· S K I M M E R S ·

Pelicans, like ospreys, terns, and other fishing birds, must see a fish before they can try to catch it. But birds called skimmers can catch fish without seeing them—even on the darkest night.

Most skimmers are less than eighteen inches long, from the top of their head to the tip of their tail. But they do have a long beak, with the lower part much longer than the upper part. So when a skimmer flies along rapidly, close to the water's surface and with its beak open, the lower part can be underwater.

When that lower part of the beak strikes a small fish, the skimmer closes its beak to grasp it. Then it gulps the fish down and flies on without stopping.

Good fishing places for skimmers are bays, creeks, and marshes. In such places a skimmer may catch a fish every few minutes. Flying close to the water, as these birds do, is called skimming. That's why they are called skimmers.

·HERONS·

Herons eat frogs, lizards, and land insects. But they also eat fish, crabs, and other small creatures found in the water. To catch them, herons make use of their long legs, long necks, and long beaks.

There are several kinds of herons. Some are no more than eighteen inches high. Others, like the great blue heron, may be over four feet tall. But all herons stand or wade about in shallow water to search for their food.

A heron may stand perfectly still in the water for a long time, watching and waiting. When a fish comes near, the heron's long neck stretches out and its head darts downward toward the fish. If it makes a catch, it raises its head, points its beak upward, and lets the fish slide down its throat. In only a few seconds it has seen the fish, caught it, and swallowed it.

When a heron sees a fish that is out of its reach, it uses another method. It seems to stand still, but it is moving forward with slow and careful steps, nearer and nearer to the fish. All at once its neck bends and—if it is fast enough—it snaps the fish up in its beak.

A heron called the reddish egret, which lives in warm southern waters, has some special tricks of its own. If there are no fish or other kinds of food in sight, it may scrape its feet rapidly over the bottom. Then, after a moment, it stops scraping and looks down to see if it has stirred up anything to eat.

Another of its tricks is to run slowly through the water with its wings partly spread out. At the sight of a school of small fish, it runs faster and spreads its wings wide. The fish dart first one way, then another. The bird runs after them.

Some of the fish may escape into water so deep that the heron can't follow them. But others may go on darting about until they tire and slow down. Then the bird stops. It spreads its wings forward and up over its head, so that they cast a dark shadow on the bottom. The tired fish, perhaps mistaking that shadow for a safe hiding place, huddle right beneath the bird. The trick has succeeded. The heron has brought the fish within easy reach of its plunging beak.

People who watch herons closely have seen a strange thing—a heron wading slowly through the water with a small feather in its beak. Suddenly the heron stops and opens its beak. The feather falls and floats on the surface of the water. A moment later a fish appears. It is swimming up from the bottom, aiming straight toward the feather. Then the heron's neck bends swiftly, and the fish is snapped up in the bird's beak.

Did the heron set a trap for the fish by dropping a feather that might look like one of the insects fish eat? It's possible.

·SANDPIPERS·

The little birds you see running swiftly up and down a beach in summer are called sandpipers. They are not swimmers, so they race ahead of incoming waves. If a wave does get close to them, they fly up into the air and flutter there a moment. Then, as the wave starts to retreat, they land again and follow it. As they run they pick up food the wave has uncovered or carried ashore.

Sandpipers use their beaks to dig into the sand in search of worms or other small creatures that live there. They also eat shrimp, mussels, and insects. And if animal food is scarce, they eat the seeds of plants.

There are many kinds of sandpipers. Some have a habit of standing on one leg when they are resting. Others have a habit of teetering back and forth. Their head dips down and their tail comes up. Then their tail dips down and their head comes up. That's why many people call these sandpipers teeter tails.

·DUCKS·

More than twenty kinds of wild ducks live on and around water and get much of their food from it. Some are no more than a foot long. Others are more than twice that size. Some live chiefly on plants, some chiefly on fish.

The handsome and very common mallard duck has a broad bill that is useful for feeding on plants that grow on the bottom of shallow creeks and bays. To reach those plants, the mallard turns upside down, leaving its tail in the air. This upside-down method of eating is called dabbling, and ducks that dabble are called dabblers.

A common fish-eating duck is the merganser. It sometimes paddles along on the surface with its head and neck stretched ahead, underwater, looking for food. Then it may suddenly leap into the air in a graceful curve and plunge underwater. It can swim rapidly, completely out of sight, after a swiftly moving fish. Its half-open wings steer it this way and that, and its paddling feet drive it along. It can fly, too, and dive down into the water from the air to make a catch.

The merganser's slender, rough-edged beak grasps a fish firmly, and the duck may swallow it whole. But if the fish is too big, the duck gulps it partway down its throat, headfirst, tail sticking out of its beak. When the head has been digested, it gulps down more of the fish, until all of it has been eaten.

· C R A B S ·

Small creatures along the shore have to do more than find the food they eat. They also have to protect themselves from being eaten. They are the natural food of seagulls, herons, and other creatures larger than they are.

The fiddler crab is one of those little creatures. It may be no larger than your fingernail and is almost never larger than your thumb. It protects itself by digging a burrow in the sand between low- and high-tide marks. The burrow looks like a hole you might make by sticking your finger in the sand, but it may be more than a foot long.

Just before the tide comes up, the crab pulls sand over the burrow entrance to seal it shut. Then water covers the entrance, and the crab is safely hidden as long as the tide is high. But when the tide goes down, the crab pushes its way out of the burrow in order to look for food along the water's edge. From that moment on, it must keep a sharp watch for enemies.

Because the crabs are so alert, you may not see a single fiddler crab as you walk past dozens of fiddler-crab holes at low tide. Before you can even get near them, the crabs have scuttled out of sight into their burrows.

But if you stand very still and watch one hole, you may soon see a claw poke out, then an eye, then a second claw. Finally the whole crab appears.

It can move sideways or forward and can move very quickly. But when the pointed ends of its eight legs feel a good patch of food, it settles down to eat.

With one claw it scoops a few grains of sand into its mouth. Inside the mouth, fine hairs with spoon-shaped tips scrape off the bits of dead plants and animals clinging to the sand. The crab swallows those bits, drops the sand, and scoops up another few grains.

The female fiddler crab uses both of its small front claws for eating. Left, right, left, right—each in turn moves up to its mouth and down again, as if the crab were keeping time to fast music.

A male fiddler crab has only one small claw that is used for eating. Its other, much larger, claw is used only for warding off a crab trying to take over its burrow, or for waving to a female crab it wants for a mate. When its claw is waving in the air, the male crab looks rather like a small, fat musician lifting up his violin—his fiddle. That's why it's called a fiddler crab.

There are many other kinds of crabs. One, the hermit crab, does not have a hard shell to protect its soft body. So it lives inside the empty shell of some other animal, often a snail. It backs into this borrowed home and hooks its rear legs onto the shell's inner wall to keep itself in place. It pokes two other pairs of legs out of the shell to move itself around. When it closes the shell's opening by folding its claws across it, it is safe from most of its enemies.

To search for food, the hermit crab unfolds its claws and pokes out its eyes, which wave about at the end of tiny stalks. If it sees bits of decaying plants or animals, it picks them up in its claws and carries them to its mouth. But it can't see very far. So if there is no food nearby, it must find it by smelling.

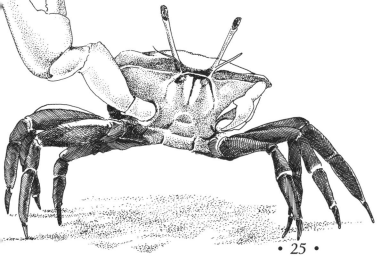

The hermit crab smells with two small, flickering feelers, each covered by hundreds of fine hairs. When it waves those feelers through the water, the hairs can pick up the smell of a dead fish or plant some distance away.

If the smell has been carried to the crab by a current of water, the crab moves against that current. As the smell grows stronger and stronger, the crab keeps moving until the food is close enough to be seen. But if there is no current in the water, the hermit crab may take a long time to find what it is smelling. It may never find that particular bit of food.

A kind of hermit crab that lives in very shallow water also has another way of getting food. It rolls over so that its legs and claws stick up out of its shell. By waving them about, it picks up the bits of food that float on the surface.

Crabs are a favorite food for many people. But it is not the little fiddler crab or the hermit crab that people enjoy. It is the larger blue crab, whose hard, bluish shell may be as much as six inches across. This crab spends its whole life underwater, where it eats almost anything—including fiddler and hermit crabs—that its powerful claws can crush or tear to pieces.

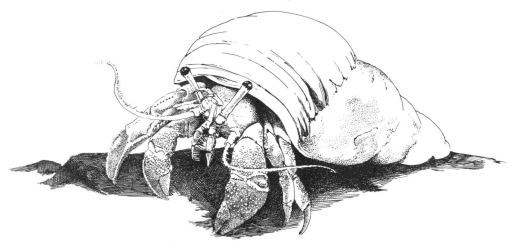

· C L A M S ·

The hard-shell clam lives underwater, too, buried just beneath a sandy or muddy bottom. Its soft body is inside a pair of hard shells that the clam makes for itself, and that grow larger every year.

A hinge joins the two shells together. By using the muscles on each side of the hinge, the clam can close the shells to protect itself. But some of its enemies are able to get the shells open and eat the clam.

One enemy is the seagull, which carries a clam high into the air and then drops it in order to break its shells.

Another is the starfish, which has its own special method of attack. The mouth of a starfish, on the underside of its body, opens straight into its baglike stomach. Its pointed arms, which surround that mouth, are very strong. When they grip a clam tightly, they force its shells to open a little. Then the starfish pushes its stomach out through its mouth and through that cracklike opening between the shells. The stomach gives off a substance that turns the clam's body into a liquid, and the starfish sucks the liquid and its own stomach back into its body.

Of course, a clam must open its own shells in order to find food. While they are open, it can thrust out the part of its body it uses as a foot and push itself along the sea bottom. But a clam never has to move to get food because it eats plankton, the tiny floating animals and plants that are found everywhere in seawater.

You can see those tiny living things only with a microscope. Among them are the larvae, or newborn babies, of many sea creatures, including clams. A young clam, in other words, is in danger of being eaten—perhaps by its own parents—from the moment it is born.

A clam gets its food by means of two tubelike parts of its body called siphons. When its shells are open, the tips of these siphons are thrust out into the water. Then waving hairs on the clam's body pull a current of plankton-filled water into one of the siphons.

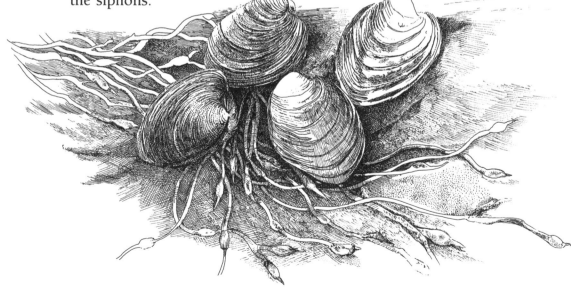

Inside the clam's body, the plankton is strained, or filtered, out of the water. More waving hairs carry the plankton along a deep groove to the clam's mouth. At the same time, the waste water is being carried out of the clam's body through the other siphon. To get the food it needs, an adult clam may pump more than fifteen quarts of water through its siphons in a single hour.

Soft-shell clams also live on plankton. And, like the hard-shell clams, they have siphons that carry seawater into and out of their bodies. But a soft-shell clam's siphons are both inside one rough, fleshy tube that is so big it can't fit inside the clam's two shells. The tube sticks out at one end, and the clam can never close its shells completely to protect itself.

To protect its soft body, the clam buries itself in the sand with its tube pointing upward. Only the tip of the tube pushes up out of the sand, allowing water to flow in and out of the clam's siphons. Once a soft-shell clam has buried itself, it stays in that place all its life.

People who like to eat these clams—some say they make the best clam chowder—search for them by looking for tiny spurts of water shooting up from the sand at low tide. Each of these fountainlike spurts is caused by a clam pumping out some of the water that carried food into its body. And each spurt tells the clam hunters that they can find a clam by digging at that spot.

·SCALLOPS·

Scallops, like clams, are among the two-shelled creatures called bivalves. And scallops also have two siphons and live on the plankton they strain out of seawater.

Empty scallop shells are easy to find on many beaches. They are marked with rays or ridges of many colors—yellow, tan, brown, gray, and orange. It is not so easy to see a live scallop. Usually it is resting on the sandy or muddy bottom of a bay or salt creek, with its shells open just enough to take in food. Sometimes scallops are so well hidden among the plants that grow on the bottom that they can't be seen at all.

A scallop does move, however, and can move very fast if necessary. By snapping its shells open and shut, open and shut, it pushes little jets of water out behind its hinge. Those jets send the scallop darting forward in little leaps.

Around the edges of the scallop's soft body is a row of blue eyes. They are so bright that they look like sapphires. With those eyes the scallop can see the shadow of an enemy floating above it and quickly close its shells or leap away.

Not everybody enjoys eating a scallop's soft gray body. But most people do like the single, small white muscle that holds the scallop's shells shut. It is so popular that in some places scallops have to be protected by law, so that they don't disappear completely. The law in those places tells people at what time of the year they may gather scallops, and how many they may gather in a day.

·MUSSELS·

The dark, oval-shaped mussel is another bivalve that lives on the plankton it strains out of the water.

When a mussel is very young, it starts to spin tough fibers, or threads, much as a spider spins threads for its web. The sticky substance at the end of those threads glues the mussel to a rock or some other hard object. And it remains there all its life, unless it is torn loose, perhaps during a storm. Then it spins new threads and settles somewhere else.

Mussels often live in clusters, or colonies, packed closely together. Sometimes they are underwater only at high tide, so only then do they open their shells to feed. At low tide, when the mussels are exposed, a seagull often tries to pick one up.

People gather mussels to cook and eat, or to use as fish bait.

·OYSTERS·

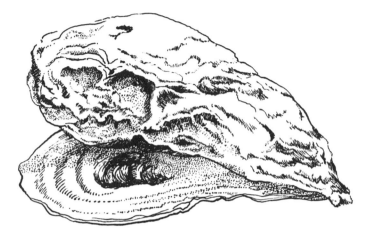

Until an oyster is about two weeks old, it looks like a pale dot floating around in the water. By then this plankton-eating bivalve has already made a tiny pair of shells that close around its soft body. At that time it gives off a substance that cements one shell to some hard object underwater—perhaps a rock or an old oyster shell. There it stays and grows, pumping water in and out of its body through its siphons. Even if you pried it loose, it would have no way of moving about.

The oyster's two worst enemies are the people who like to eat it and a small grayish snail less than an inch long. That snail also eats mussels and other shelled creatures. But it attacks so many oysters, by a process called drilling, that it is known as the oyster drill.

· S N A I L S ·

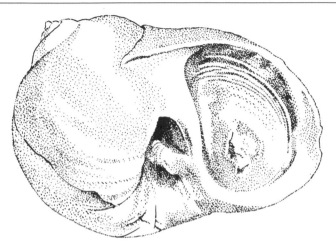

Like most snails, the oyster drill protects its soft body inside a spiral-shaped shell it builds for itself. An opening on the side of its shell lets it thrust out a siphon, a broad foot, and its head. On that head are two pointed stalks called tentacles, with eyes at their tips. Between them is a long, tubelike snout shaped rather like an elephant's trunk. Inside the snout is the snail's drilling tool, called a radula. The radula looks like a stiff ribbon, with hard teeth at the center and rows of softer teeth on either side.

If you could watch exactly what happens when an oyster drill attacks an oyster, this is what you would see.

The oyster drill finds its prey by smelling the waste water pumped out of the oyster's body. It creeps slowly up onto the oyster's rough shell. For as long as half an hour, it moves around there. It is feeling the shell's surface with its snout, choosing the place for its drilling. It may settle upon a spot where there is already a tiny crack.

There, through its foot, the snail spreads an acid that can dissolve shell. Then it thrusts the radula out of its snout, pushing it over the surface of the oyster shell. As the radula moves, it scrapes off tiny bits of softened shell. The bits are so small that they could be seen only through a microscope. Then the radula is pulled back.

Again and again, the radula moves forward and back. Very slowly it is wearing away the shell that is softened by the acid the snail keeps on producing.

An oyster drill usually has to work for at least three days before it drills a hole all the way through the shell. Then its snout stretches down through that hole, and with the soft teeth on the radula the snail begins to eat the oyster. A few hours later, or perhaps not until several days have passed, the oyster shell is completely empty.

There are many different kinds of snails. Not all of them have a snout like the oyster drill. But all of them have an opening along one side of their shell, which can be sealed off by the tough plate at the end of the snail's foot. That plate is called an operculum. When the operculum opens, like a door, the foot and the snail's head, which is attached to it, poke out.

The most common snails are the ordinary mud snails. They are dark in color and about half an inch long. They crawl slowly about on their foot, looking for food on a muddy or sandy sea bottom. A mud snail's wide mouth, between its two tentacles, will swallow almost anything.

If a fisherman drops the skeleton of a cleaned fish into the water, it will soon be buried under an army of snails. In a short time, the snails will clean off and swallow every bit of flesh clinging to the bones.

One of the chief enemies of these mud snails is the blue crab. Its powerful claws can crush the snail's shell and pick out the soft body inside. To escape a crab, a snail will climb up a blade of the tall marsh grass that grows along the shores of creeks and bays. At high tide, when the water has risen partway up the grass and crabs are swimming about in it, a snail will climb to the very top of a blade. There it is safe from its enemies, which are only a few inches below. And it can cling so tightly to its perch that even a strong breeze can't blow it off or shake it loose.

·BARNACLES·

Did you ever pick up a rock at the water's edge and find it covered with what looked like rough white dots? Did you look closely at those dots, some no bigger than a pinhead?

Each dot is a tiny animal called an acorn shell or sea acorn. Acorn shells belong to a family of sea creatures known as barnacles, whose soft bodies are protected by shells made up of several pieces. Through a magnifying glass, an acorn shell looks like a miniature volcano made of six or more overlapping shells. Like a volcano, it has a hole or crater at the top. And inside the crater there are four more shells, each hinged to the volcano's inside wall.

When the tide covers this barnacle, those four shells stand open, much like the petals of an open tulip. In that position they let water into the shell, and the barnacle can get its food.

The barnacle's body, inside its shell, looks something like a shrimp. It lies on its back, with its feet poking upward. There are fringes of hair at the ends of those feet. As the feet wave about in the water, the hairs trap plankton and other bits of food and wave them into the barnacle's mouth. One scientist said that at high tide barnacles are "kicking their food into their mouth."

As the tide goes down, the four little shells click shut, forming a neat cap over the crater and sealing a drop of water inside the shell. That keeps the barnacle from drying out before the tide covers it again.

If you stand beside a big, barnacle-covered rock as the tide is falling and put your ear close to it, you might hear those shells clicking shut. Thousands of them clicking together make a soft sound that has been called the whispering talk of barnacles.

·SEA SQUIRTS·

The sea squirt is shaped like a round, well-filled bag, with one opening at its top and another at its side. Some sea squirts never grow larger than a pea. Other kinds grow as large as your fist. A large sea squirt, some people say, looks like a knobby, grayish potato.

A sea squirt lives at the low-tide line or just below it, fastened to a rock or some other hard object. Waving hairs inside its body force water and plankton into the top opening and through a clothlike strainer. The plankton is trapped by a sticky substance and swallowed. The strained water leaves by the side opening. As much as forty-five gallons of water a day can pass through a sea squirt no bigger than a small potato.

If it is touched or squeezed, water squirts out of both of a sea squirt's openings. That's why this curious creature was given its curious name.

·JELLYFISH·

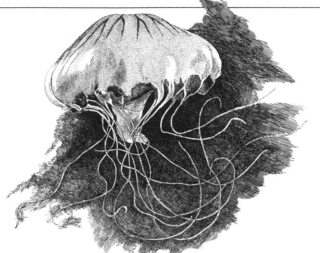

A jellyfish doesn't look at all like a fish. But it does look very much like jelly—a round blob of it that may be pinkish or purplish or brown. Long threads hang down from its ruffled edges. Some jellyfish are smaller than the palm of your hand, others as large as a dinner plate. But even a small jellyfish can have long threads, or tentacles. On a Portuguese man-of-war, a deepwater jellyfish, they are sometimes ten feet long.

Around the edge of the jellyfish are the muscles that move it through the water. They do this by curling the edge down and under and then pushing it up and out again. A moving jellyfish looks like an umbrella that someone is closing, opening, and then closing again.

Those long, hanging threads can find and capture small fish and the tiny animals in plankton. When one of them brushes against a small fish, it sends out a tiny sharp hook, or barb. The barb pierces a hole in the fish's skin and sends a drop of poison into the hole. The poison paralyzes the fish. Some jellyfish threads can also send out fine sticky hairs that hold a fish until the poison can do its work.

As soon as the fish is helpless, the threads carry it to an opening in the underside of the jellyfish. That opening, at the very center of the jellylike blob, is the jellyfish's mouth.

No one who goes swimming in seawater wants to be touched by a jellyfish. The poison in its tentacles can make skin red, itchy, and hot. Some people even become very ill from brushing against jellyfish in the water.

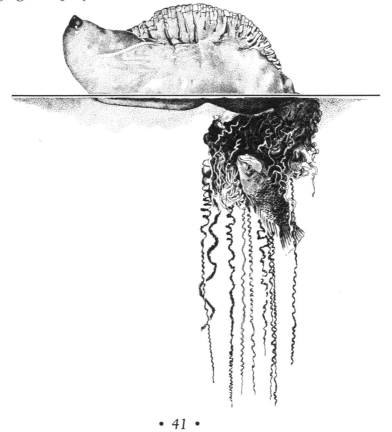

· C O M B J E L L I E S ·

Comb jellies are relatives of the jellyfish. Their bodies also look as if they were made of jelly. But in their case the jelly is not colored. Instead it is as clear and transparent as a piece of glass. Most comb jellies are no larger than a lemon and may be smaller. They may be sausage shaped or as round as a ball.

A comb jelly's mouth is at one end of its body, between a pair of long, dangling threads. And running along its body are the combs that give it its name. Each comb is a row of upright hairs that glisten in sunlight and reflect the colors of the rainbow. Those waving hairs move the comb jelly through the water.

When one of the long threads touches a bit of animal food in plankton, it produces a sticky substance that holds the food fast. After the thread has collected several bits of food, it moves forward to the front of the comb jelly's body to wipe the food off into its mouth.

·CORALS·

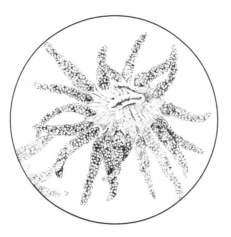

The tiny coral is also related to the jellyfish. It, too, has a soft, bloblike body edged with threads. But its body is shaped like a cup, with its threads rising from the top, and it builds a hard wall around itself. As generations of coral live and die, their walls are left standing. And billions of them, packed closely together, form the steadily growing coral reefs found along tropical shores.

Corals use their threads to trap plankton for food, but there is very little plankton in their warm-water home. So no one could understand, for a long time, how corals could grow there and build all those sturdy walls. Then scientists discovered that tiny plants live inside these tiny creatures and help supply what they need. The plants give off sugar, which the corals use as food. The plants also provide much of the hard substance, called calcium, with which the corals build their walls.

·WORMS

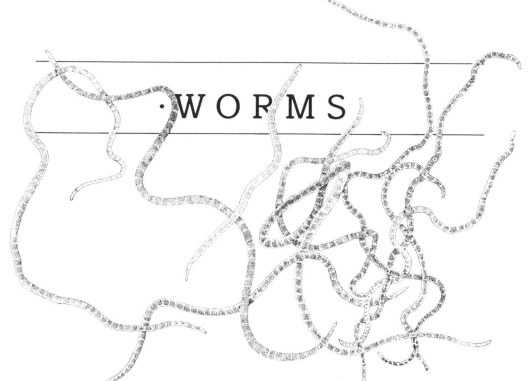

Many kinds of worms live in the water, or so close to it that they are underwater at high tide. Some are excellent swimmers and dart about like fish. Some crawl along the sand or mud. Others spend their lives in tunnels they dig in the sea bottom.

Each worm has its own way of getting food. Some pump water through their bodies and filter plankton out of it, in much the same way shellfish do. Some just swallow the sand they are digging through. Their stomachs digest the tiny bits of dead plants and animals stuck to the grains of sand, and then those grains pass on through their bodies.

The sandworm, one of the burrow-digging worms, can also swim and crawl about under rocks and among water plants. Its powerful jaws can rip off pieces of seaweed and tear up bits of dead animals and other food it finds.

The bloodworm digs a whole network of tunnels, with several entrances into it from the water above. As it digs, the bloodworm gives off a substance that forms a lining for its tunnels.

Water flows into those tunnels through the many entrances. Other creatures enter the tunnels through those entrances, too. Another worm might come in, searching for food. Or a small shellfish might poke through one of the openings. The bloodworm is waiting for just such a visitor.

While it waits, it keeps its head tucked inside its body, like the toe of a sock turned outside in. The instant another creature enters its network of tunnels, the bloodworm knows it because the new arrival changes the pressure of the water against the bloodworm's body. So the bloodworm starts toward the intruder with its feelers out and its powerful jaws ready to attack. Rows of small arms on each side of its body move it along by pushing against the smooth tunnel walls.

As soon as its feelers touch its prey, the bloodworm's jaws thrust forward, grasp the visitor, and inject it with poison. When the visitor has stopped struggling, the bloodworm eats it on the spot.

The jaws of both bloodworms and sandworms are ready to nip the hand of any person who picks them up. But fishermen like to use them both for bait, and they learn to handle them carefully. Professional worm-diggers dig up and sell millions of these worms every year.

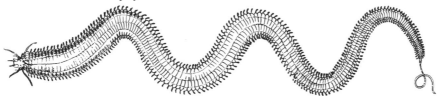

Have you been surprised by some of the eating habits of the sea-shore creatures—the fliers, the swimmers, the water pumpers, the crawlers, and the burrowers? Now if you go to the beach for a picnic lunch, do you think you could find food there as cleverly as they do? Or will you stick to the usual habit of human beings, and take along some sandwiches for your lunch?

·Index·

acorn shells, 37–38

barnacles, 37–38
bays, 17, 21, 30, 36
beaks, 9, 13–14, 15–16, 17, 22
bivalves, 30, 32, 33
bloodworms, 44–45
blue crabs, 26, 36

calcium, 43
clam chowder, 29
clams, 9, 27–29, 30
claws, 24–25, 26
comb jellies, 42
corals, 43
crabs, 10, 23–26, 36
creeks, 17, 21, 30, 36

dabblers, 21
digestion, 22, 28–29
ducks, 21–22

eggs, 10

fiddler crabs, 23–25, 26
fish, 10, 11–19, 21–22, 36, 40–41
fishermen, 10, 14, 29, 32, 36, 45
fish hawks, 11–12
frogs, 11, 18

garbage, 10
great blue herons, 18
grubs, 10